MARVELOUS MAMMALS

by John Stewart

SCHOOL PUBLISHERS

Cover, ©Chris Howes/Wild Places Photography/Alamy; p.2, ©blickwinkel/Alamy; p.3, ©Stephen Frink/CORBIS; p.4, The Image Bank/Cousteau Society/Getty Images; p.5, ©Garry Gay/Alamy; p.6, ©Jeff Foott/Discovery Channel Images/Getty Images; p.7, ©Jeff Foott/Getty Images; p.8, ©Jon Sergison/Alamy; p.9, ©Kevin Schafer/Corbis; p.10, ©Stuart Westmorland/Getty Images; p.11, ©Danita Delimont/Alamy Images; p.12, ©Royalty-Free/Corbis; p.13, ©Andy Holligan/Getty Images; p.14, ©Harcourt Telescope.

Printed in China

ISBN 10: 0-15-350558-3
ISBN 13: 978-0-15-350558-4

Ordering Options
ISBN 10: 0-15-350335-1 (Grade 5 Below-Level Collection)
ISBN 13: 978-0-15-350335-1 (Grade 5 Below-Level Collection)
ISBN 10: 0-15-357559-X (package of 5)
ISBN 13: 978-0-15-357559-4 (package of 5)

4 5 6 7 8 9 10   0940   12 11 10 09

Motorboats like the one in this photograph can hurt a manatee or sea otter.

Marvelous mammals dwell beneath the ocean's surface. It's sad that some of these interesting creatures—like manatees and sea otters—have become endangered. Human actions are threatening these members of the large marine ecosystem. What makes these animals special? How are they different from other creatures? Let's find out the answers to these questions.

Manatees

Manatees are mammals that spend their lives in the water. People might mistake them for large, slow, chubby seals. They can grow as long as 15 feet (4.6 m). They can weigh as much as 3,500 pounds (1,588 kg). They eat plants. Sometimes they can be seen basking in the shallow freshwater of a river. However, manatees are able to live in salt water as well. They might also be seen in oceans not far from the shore.

Manatees are shaped like very big sausages. They have no back legs or flippers. Their front limbs appear too short for their bodies. Still, they are very useful. A manatee often feeds on floating vegetation. Those short flippers have claws to help grip any plant the manatee might detect. Manatees use their odd lips to move the plants into their mouths. Each lip is split in the middle. The sides of each lip can move independently, almost like thumbs.

Manatees are eating machines that can eat up to 150 pounds (68 kg) of plants each day. They spend a lot of time nibbling at the bottom of shallow waters. If the water is clear enough for you to see them, they might remind you of grazing cattle. That's why manatees are sometimes called "sea cows." They are not closely related to cows, though. In fact, their closest land cousin is the elephant.

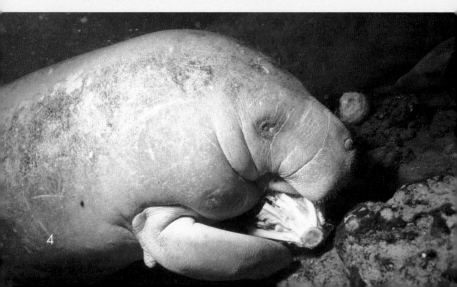

Manatees have a special trait that no other animal shares:"marching molars." Because they spend so much time chewing their food, their front molars, or teeth, wear down quickly. No problem! Their back teeth on each side of the jaw are growing all the time. When a front molar gets too worn to work well, it falls out—and the rest of the molars move forward, one by one,"marching" neatly into their new place. A replacement molar begins to grow right away in the "hole" left in the back of the row.

Manatees have big heads, but their eyes are small. They do not see very well underwater. Their hearing is good, even though their ears look like mere pinholes. Because a manatee is a mammal, fresh air is vital for its survival. It breathes through a snout that sits high on its head. It just has to stick its nostrils out of the water to take a breath. These nostrils have valves to let air in—and to keep water out. When a manatee sinks below the surface, it shuts the valves. Although they can stay underwater for around twenty minutes if they have to, manatees usually come up for air every five minutes or so.

Manatees have few natural predators because of their size. Then why are they facing the threat of becoming extinct? Humans are their greatest enemy. Hunters are only a small part of the problem. People hit manatees by accident with speedboats. People drown them by accident when they catch them in commercial fishing nets. Manatees may die when they try to eat fishhooks or trash that people have tossed aside. Worst of all, people are destroying their home. There are just a few thousand manatees left in the wild, and their numbers are going down. If people don't protect them, they could vanish from the face of the earth.

Sea Otters

The smallest of all marine mammals is the sea otter. It can weigh up to about 88 pounds (40 kg). It can grow to be about four feet (1.2 m) long from the top of its head to the tip of its tail. Like all marine mammals, sea otters must keep warm. They do not have huge amounts of body fat like other mammals do. Instead, these sleek creatures have the densest fur in the world. You wouldn't want to have to count their hairs. There are up to one million of them per square inch.

Sea otters float on their backs much of the time, even when eating, resting, or sleeping. To move through the water more quickly, they turn over onto their stomachs. Then they propel themselves with their hind legs. Their webbed feet act as flippers. Their long, flattened tails help them steer.

Even though they have all that dense hair, sea otters must still be careful not to get too cold. They are very active. This keeps their body temperature up. Another way they fight the cold is by eating plenty of clams, crabs, octopuses, sea urchins, snails, fish, and other sea creatures.

At mealtime, the sea otter uses tools. Underwater, the clever creature knows that a rock is a great tool for separating an abalone from its protective shell. It might also put a flat stone under its arm and carry it to the surface. Floating on its back, the sea otter places the flat stone on its chest. The stone acts as a perfect hard surface on which to pound a clam or mussel until the shell breaks. As far as scientists know, sea otters are the only mammals besides primates that make use of tools.

Sea otters live in groups called "rafts." Sometimes rafts have as many as a hundred members. When it's not mating season, males and females separate. Their rafts go to different resting areas. A raft stays together much of the time. The otters even sleep side by side. To prevent themselves from drifting away from their raft, they often wrap their bodies in kelp, a kind of seaweed which acts as an anchor.

A sea otter has two layers of fur. The hairs on the layer closest to the body are very fine and trap air. The warmth from the sea otter's body heats this air and protects the animal from the cold water. The top layer of fur is made up of "guard hairs." These hairs are long and waterproof and protect the *underlayer*—as long as they stay clean! That's why sea otters spend almost half their day cleaning themselves. They use their front claws to rake through their hair and get foreign particles out.

Scientists think that there used to be about 300,000 sea otters along the northern Pacific coastlines. Two hundred years ago, this population ranged from Japan and Russia to Alaska and California. However, if you analyzed human activity in the last two centuries, you would learn some very sad facts. From the mid-1700s until 1911, these lively creatures were hunted almost to extinction for their unique fur.

Finally, in 1911, an international treaty banned the trade of sea otter fur. Since then, the sea otter population has been slowly climbing again. However, there are other dangers from humans, such as oil spills. If oil gets into an otter's fur, it sticks to the underlayer. This pops the air bubbles that protect the otter's body from the cold water. It might die from the cold before it is able to clean the oil from its fur. Oil spills can take the lives of thousands of otters.

Fortunately, people are taking steps to prevent any further damage to endangered marine mammals like sea otters and manatees. All people must learn how their own actions can affect the environment of marine mammals in a negative way. Then people must be careful to avoid those actions. If people stay alert, all these marvelous creatures will continue to survive.

Think Critically

1. Why has the population of sea otters declined so much over the past two hundred years?

2. Why does a sea otter groom its fur much of the time?

3. Which animals do you think are more interesting— manatees or sea otters? Explain your answer.

4. What is the author's purpose in writing this book?

5. Why are manatees facing the danger of becoming extinct?

 **Science**

More Marine Mammals When somebody thinks about mammals, they usually think about land animals. However, there are many mammals that actually live in the water. Conduct research on the Internet to find information on several other mammals that live in the ocean, lakes, or rivers. Make a chart comparing facts about these animals.

School-Home Connection Share this book with a family member. Then discuss what it would be like to see a manatee or a sea otter in person. What might you see each animal doing?

Word Count: 1,279